What Word for This

What Word for This

poems

Marion Starling Boyer

GRAYSON BOOKS
West Hartford, Connecticut
graysonbooks.com

What Word for This
copyright © 2023 by Marion Starling Boyer
published by Grayson Books
West Hartford, Connecticut
ISBN: 979-8-9855442-7-5

Book and Cover Design: Cindy Stewart
Cover Photo: Barbara Sabol
Author Photo: Thanks to Melanie Rae Buonavolonta

The sound of the wind through trees
is called *psithurism*.
There's no word for the translator of wind.
If the wind is words, the trees are exclamation points.
The spears of moonlight, question marks.

—Victoria Chang

Contents

Komorebi

*Japanese for sunbeams piercing
through branches in dense woods*

Suddenness filled our separate worlds
the day I saw the fox and the fox saw me.

Her tapered nose quivered
and the space between us hummed.

I hollowed myself to go still.
It was green moment, pure

as shafts of light fingering
through leaf lace in a forest

until her body shifted and the air
became brittle as film ice.

On legs of smoke she sped,
her russet tail a streamer in the underbrush.

Cento For Mångata

Swedish for the moon's reflection on water
making a shining pathway to the horizon

The deepest part of night.
Shoulder to tender shoulder, you say,

    tell me a make-believe.

I start imagining possibilities.

A shopkeeper would go down to the beach.
He studied the brilliant white mystery
of moonlight floating on the lake.

He learned that sticking spoons
in the garden attracted moonlight.

    Like moon-tug, you say.

His collection, a bag of tiny moons
he jingled in his pocket, disappears.

Wherever I am going with the story,
it's opening its wings.

    Tell me about his lost moons.

The night is ours. Easy enough to imagine
we have time.

Luminous. Miraculous. That's what he said.
Many of them copper-colored.

He does not remember how he lost them.
He said it was a relief.
There were too many of them.

Every cell of your being responds
as something heavy lifts, slow as smoke,
slow as steam off a bath.

Culaccino

Italian word for ring-shaped stains left by a wet glass

I know a few tricks to remove the white rings
sweaty glasses leave on polished tabletops:
a hairdryer on low, a light buff with extra fine
steel wool or mayonnaise rubbed into the grain.

My mother and grandmothers kept their dining room
tables shining. For company, the table was protected
by a thick, custom-made pad and pressed tablecloth.
Our family guards a glossy surface.

In rainswept Scottish glens more than five
thousand years ago, humans hunched over
flat tables of sandstone to peck patterns
of cups and rings into the rock.

Cups and rings, circles within circles were carved
in stone on every continent people have lived.
I've seen on the face of one sandstone rock in Utah's
canyonlands thousands of petroglyphs—

antelope, buffalo, men on horseback, bighorn sheep
and circles like wheels, circles that spiral, rings
like water rippling—each carving an anecdote
of ancient triumphs, of tribal news.

I wish now for a long wooden table handed down
by my people. I want its surface littered with rings
left when the family gathered, laughing, feasting.
I want rings to mark my mother's grief, some emblem

for the time we lost my infant sister, Joan. The death
we could never speak about. White rings in the wood
from late night brooding over bills, from too much drink,
every dull halo from our wet glasses overflowing.

Iktsuarpok

*Inuit for repeatedly going outside to check for someone's
anticipated arrival*

When I drive I-80 to my mother's, somewhere before Gary's
smokestacks and the hellbent traffic ringing Chicago, time folds
and I am given eleven to noon over again. In that hour, restless,
she'll abandon the newspaper puzzle, smooth a cushion, check the
window. The kitchen table will be laid for lunch, sandwiches under
a damp tea towel. Napkins triangled.

As her anxiety ratchets, all within her will lean east, stretch down
the street toward the highway. This is when I always call. Her
hello tight, buzzy. I'll say, *Hi Mom. I'm an hour away* and hear
her inhale, then brittle-bright, *I'm so glad you called, dear. Please
be careful.* I'll answer, *I will. Love you* and she'll breathe, *love you
too, dear.* In this hour we are best at loving each other. While the
time zones bleed together we rehearse our frost-tender smiles, plan
to begin over again.

white cyclamen
on the polished table
one leaf yellowing

Nyepi

Balinese National Day of Silence
honoring the Hindu New Year

In two wing beats, the pileated woodpecker glides
to the woods where I have seen his mate.

January first. My world is muffled in snow.

A sparrow scallops the air. A few finches, their yellow
muted by winter, wing feeder to feeder.

The snow begins to fall again. I imagine the birds'
hunger, imagine them late in the night
huddled deep in pockets of pine and spruce,

hearts slowed, bony feet gripping boughs, waiting
for the Earth to revolve again toward the light,

spin silent in space, quiet as snow settling on snow.

L'appel Du Vide

French for an irrational impulse to jump from a height

I jog the track above basketball courts
keeping my distance from the waist-high wall.
The overlook is magnetic. Invisible hands reach
for me. A breath at the ear: *Come on. Lean over.*

Today, I hear no balls thunk the backboards,
no sneaker squeaks. The gym below is empty
except for a baton twirler. She's a bright jack
tumbling on the floor. Her baton pops up.

Once, at Niagara Falls, Dad posed me for a photo
at the lip. The glassy water surged over,
down to white billows, urging: *Just step in.*

The twirler's baton spins to the ceiling lights.
I slow and watch her whip her body into
a windmill then catch it blind behind her back.
I see too, half her face is burn-scarred.

In Colorado last year, while my skis dangled
beneath me on the chairlift, I fixed my eyes
on lodgepole pines, gripped the seat. As I brushed
by treetops, snow broke from the branches,
showered down. Wind coaxed: *It's easy. Slip off.*

The twirler rehearses elbow rolls, flips the baton
around her neck, tosses it, cartwheels, captures it,
whirls. She trusts herself in ways I haven't found.
See now—how she flings her body into the world.

Adjal

Indonesian for one's predestined day of death

Conversations remain eye level in the locker room
where I dress after swimming. Metal doors clank.
Someone frets about icy roads. A waft of lotion.

I knock water from my ears. Duffels zip. The door opens
to humid air saturated in chlorine and a young woman
comes in from the pool, strips her speedo for the showers.

She's the swimmer who had knifed the surface, lap after lap,
flip-turning like a machine while next to her I side-stroked
and twice dipped underwater to run my hand along the blue
lane stripe, then surfaced, gasping.

Now I plug in my hairdryer while an aisle over
a white-haired woman grips her towel and twirls the padlock
again, panic ticking like a beetle in her wrist.

Warm air on my neck calls back a memory of being small,
sitting in the shade, sipping Orange Crush from a glass bottle
through a straw. *Click.* The woman yanks her lock open,
drops to the bench.

As I walk to my car a thought strikes me, true as a cast bell:
The day I die it will be snowing, everything white and blurred.
Wet tatters fall from a tissue paper sky,
same as the day I was born.

Poronkusema

Finnish word to describe roughly five miles,
based on the habits of reindeer

Arctic herders measured distance by how long
a traveling reindeer could hold its water.

Every animal has its limits. A *furlong* was how far an ox
could plough a furrow without rest. Eight furlongs equaled

an "old London" mile. Like magic beans, an idea roots
in my son's mind: he will run a one-hundred-mile race.

My son, who has never been an athlete, never a runner,
begins training. Then, in the pre-dawn darkness,

his ultra-race starts like a legend at Squires Castle,
which is, in fact, in Cleveland.

He runs into the day—runs furlongs, a marathon. Two.
The crowd cheers and claps. Cow bells clank.

The Finns have another word for how far a dog's bark
carries in the still air. We sort mystery by measuring it.

At twelve *poronkusema* we weep when my son bursts
from the forest to a meadow and fist-pumps.

At mile seventy-one he is whittled, battered. Stoic.
I can't imagine how he continues on.

For whatever lies beyond our understanding
we weave myths. At the map's edge we draw dragons;

we say the sun returns after the long winter nights
because the Reindeer Mother flies it back in her antlers.

Well after midnight, at mile ninety-three we wait,
slumped in canvas chairs at an empty lot behind a car wash.

Here he seems to shatter, then shuffles on.
At twenty-three hours eighteen minutes my son finishes

and folds down. Every animal has its limits.
He can recount numbers to describe his race; miles,

increments of time, but I can't hold them in my mind.
I make sense the way a Finnish mother does, pointing

up to the aurora's light, telling her child it is sparks
thrown from a fox's tail as he races across the night.

Boketto

Japanese for gazing vacantly into the distance

Drifting up through grey fog, everything soft,
our airplane rises to the vault of blue above
a blanket of clouds like carded wool. Below,
rivers, lakes, the patchwork of place erased.

Airplane hum. My mind an empty vault. Above
the clouds, I gaze out the window seeing nothing.
Rivers, lakes, patchwork farmlands all erased.
My dad would say I was woolgathering

when I gazed out the car window, seeing nothing.
In his last years, when his memory was in shreds,
Dad would wander like a woolgatherer
plucking tufts snagged in thorny brush.

Last year I put away my memory of him
staring vacantly while we tried to distract him
from plucking at his skin like a thorny problem.
Instead, I fix my mind on his smile, teasing

me for staring vacantly out a window. Distracted
by these clouds, clean as carded wool below,
nothing remains fixed in my mind. Even his smile
drifts now through grey fog, everything soft.

Buddhi

Sanskrit for intuitive knowledge of such certainty
it is a state of being

Every time Imogene Conner opened her door
instead of *hello*, she asked, *Well, what do you know for sure?*

and I always came up empty. Some scientist determined dust
clouds in the Milky Way would taste of raspberries

and another says koalas have fingerprints nearly identical
to humans, but what if Imogene wanted to know something

soul-deep true, like Elaine's conviction when she first met Bill,
that she'd marry him. Like Edgar Mitchell, who looked at

earth from space and *knew* life in our universe is not random.
Like Amanda's certainty that she's lived several previous lives

and in each her mother was someone close but not her mother.
Once, on trip to Egypt, Amanda entered a tomb

and remembered she'd been locked there as a slave.
The tour director had to ease her outside as she sobbed.

Imogene died over two decades ago but I still see her,
leaning against the screen door. I still hear her voice asking.

Yoin

Japanese for an experience that lingers in memory long afterwards

We were four women walking the beach after midnight,
our feet sinking in the cool sand, listening to the ocean expand

and recede in the dark. We'd flown to Florida to briefly escape
our separate lives: one from her troubled marriage,

another from the demands of children, the third still mourning
a miscarriage, and the fourth, a different death.

We talked softly. Small holes in the sand burbled and spit. A ghost
crab skittered sideways like an arthritic hand running piano keys.

In the moonlight a reptilian body emerged, large as a manhole
cover, dripping foam. A sea turtle come home to lay her eggs.

She labored, scraping toward sea grapes and grasses well above
the tideline. We made a broad space, then waited like midwives

as the turtle swept sand behind her, dug a hole with her flippers.
The work was hard. She strained her head forward, the folds

of her neck stretched smooth, jaws opening. She gasped.
Groaned. Heaved sand shoulder high, flinging left and right.

Whumps from her rocking shell shuddered the ground.
The sea smoothed onto the beach, shushed back to itself.

She expelled the eggs beneath her and rested before ploughing
sand into a crest over them with her flippers.

Like a shell pocketed from the beach, we each carried that night
differently, returning to our lives—how the turtle used her nose

to anchor in, to drag forward by inches before melting
into the water, the mound she abandoned large as a human grave.

Cento For Yūgen

*Japanese for an awareness of the universe that evokes
emotions too profound and mysterious to express.*

look at the Moon
        silver
it floats in silence
in eternal cold

I am one of the lucky ones
to see the Moon
        close up
I tell you
until I saw Earth from space
I never knew what round meant

        the bright Earth
            pretty and blue
        slow-swirling veils of white
in blackness, emptiness
beyond imagination

        delicate clean
        my God, I thought
        touch it and it would crumble

everything dear
everyone you love
every human who ever was
        suspended there

our tiny world
        alone in a sunbeam

and the Sun
less than halfway through its life
            ripens a bunch of grapes
as if it has nothing else to do.

Saudade

Portuguese word meaning desire
for what one does not have
or nostalgia for what one has never had

Paris. Late. I'm seated in a candle-lit restaurant.
White linens. It doesn't have to be Paris. Chicago.

Chicago, when the air is warm. I'm drinking
a dirty martini. I want to remember wearing

stilettos, a red dress when he moves toward me,
his eyes embers. I want to miss that. And flinging

a glass to smash against the wall. An upended table.
A Times-Square, V-J Day, bent back kiss. That too.

Instead, I met and married the guy. Had two sons.
Paid the bills, voted. Baked brownies. No furies.

No rain-sobbing, everything cold and choked. My story
is not a brown fur of sorrow draped around my neck

like a mink, its mouth clenching its tail. Nothing silver
screen. We rake leaves. We watch sunsets. We save up

for trips. We kiss goodnight. He is my one. My only.
And I am his. So shouldn't we have learned to tango,

to hold one another in the frame, spines straight, my arm
stretching elegant to my fingertips in a fan step?

Our torsos would lunge and rotate, *slow-slow*, our legs
flick *quick-quick*, and then, *slow*, my leg hooks around his.

Yr

Norwegian for foggy drizzle, heavy mist

Our train car sways, rumbles alongside
the tumbling Rio Urubamba.

Even the river's name cascades—
say *Urubamba.*

We arrive in a cloud forest.
Machu Picchu clings to a mountain

in thin air. Fog bathes rhododendrons.
Llamas graze the green terraces.

Our guide, Roberto, leads us up stone steps
to the Temple of the Sun. Mist moves

through the valley, milky wisps
float among the mountains.

I am so very far from home.
I put my hand on a wet stone wall.
There are no ghosts here.

Roberto cannot say why the Inca
were here, only that they were,

like dreams you nearly recall before they lift.
In the history of my people, our minds age

into cloud forests. We cannot say when
it will happen, only that, slowly, it will.

When the fog comes whispering for me,
which memories will cling? My husband's face.

A phrase of music. The yeasty warmth of bread.
The sound of a river, tumbling. *Urubamba*.

Nepakartojama

Lithuanian word for a never-to-be-
replicated, perfect experience

We sail to the Galapagos
where black-winged frigates soar

high overhead in warlike formations
against the blue, blue sky.

In the scuff on Española island
a male frigate throws back his head,

balloons his red throat pouch
and shimmies his long wings.

A drumming comes from his bill
until a mate slides her bill into his

and in rhythms that are theirs alone
they snake their heads together.

Here, blue-footed boobies stare down
their long bills at us, slightly cross-eyed

and the air above the sea beats
with swooping flocks of them.

Suddenly, a whole cloud of boobies
pivot to wing point, aim,

plunge like missiles,
bomb the water.

How we pour ourselves into bird.
Oh! how our sore hearts rise

as an albatross skims
the windward side of a wave,

carries his burden of luck
straight into the sun.

Vedriti

*Slovenian for taking shelter from the rain
or waiting out a difficult situation*

The Kenyan road is deeply rutted. Our jeep sways and bounces around potholes large as bushel baskets. We reach a market with concrete shops painted blue, lime, orange; a red building plastered with Coca-Cola logos, the white script luminous against the leaden sky. Women in long skirts select beans. Men toe the dirt, talking.

dusty earth
scent of old blood
and potatoes

Then down comes rain, drumming the jeep. Rain hammers the hard ground, races from corrugated metal roofs. Mud streams, water pools ankle-deep. Shoppers squeeze in doorways, under awnings. Our jeep stops when a matatu slews around a curve. Arms branch from its windows; one man clings on, half out of the crammed taxi-van. I lift my camera.

the flamingos
return to Lake Nakuru—
a watermelon cracks open

A man shouts, pointing. Eyes swing toward me. A woman, two other men point, yell. People in doorways unclot from their shelter. My friends cry out, *put it away, put your camera away!* Our jeep lurches forward, rocks left, then right. Colors blur.

afternoon light
savanna grass
becomes a lion

Forelsket

Danish for the euphoric feeling of falling in love

He is a boy, perhaps fourteen. A boy in Florence, just before the city lights the evening. The air scented with rinsed pavement. The boy sprints down the sidewalk. At the streetlamp he vaults, grasps the post one-handed, and spins to round the corner. A grey man in a grey coat turns to watch him spring onto a park bench, feather step its length, and bound away.

bells pealing
from the duomo tower
an explosion of wings

Zwischenraum

German word for intervals or space between things

The taped lines on the floor of the grocery's checkout lanes
are a year old now. We are still polite, distancing.

I swam at the rec center today. Three of us were allowed
thirty minutes in the cavernous space. The other woman

backstroked, flicking her hands up crisply while the man
dropped his arms like shovels.

The volume of warm air was still. The volume of water
barely stirred.

I've grown accustomed to vacancy, sky
where the maple came down; absence heavy as the empty chair;

the pause of an ellipsis after *I need to tell you something...*
When a jigsaw piece is lost it's hard to see anything but that void.

Summer nights in Tennessee the insect lady can identify species
of lightning bugs by the intervals between their flashes

and can locate where you call home if you say they're fireflies.
There's a place in the Smoky Mountains where fireflies blink

in unison. The forest twinkles everywhere at once, goes black,
then the starry lights again search out each other in the dark.

I'm missing something deep, something nearly tribal
that's in the way Greeks clasp shoulders, grapevine

slowly, then faster, beaming in each other's sweaty faces;
how in dark theaters we become one animal breathing.

Back when Janice told us about her brain cancer we could cluster
tight around her. Faithful and faithless, we all bent forward

reaching to touch her or rest a hand on one nearer.
We were fireflies crowded in a mason jar, glowing like a lantern.

Tingo

*Rapa Nui word for the Easter Island custom
of taking a friend's admired possessions
until the friend is left with nothing*

Jane's nephew intends to be a monk.
I just need someone to take care of my food

and waste, he says. And I read a retired
couple has rid themselves of everything

to live entirely on cruise ships. *It's cheaper
than a mortgage and groceries,* they claim.

This urge toward minimalism seduces me.
I welcome *tingo* since inheriting silver-

plated flatware, porcelain figurines, assorted
silk ties, several sets of china, twenty tea pots,

a slide projector, and a Victrola. Admire any
of these and, bingo, they're yours. Bring a truck.

I'd been acting like a hermit crab, shucking
my shell for the next more capacious one

and now the things I own seem to own me.
The shift was gradual. I acquired stuff the way

a clownfish, swishing through anemones, acquires
an isopod. The isopod slips in through his gills

and is accommodated on the clownfish's tongue.
But, over time, the isopod grows legs and embraces

the tongue, tight as envy, until the tongue wastes away.
Maybe I've grown so attached to things I've become

the clownfish who cannot live without the isopod
acting as his new living tongue.

Uitwaaien

Dutch for walking in the wind to whisk the mind clean

People have been swept off this pier and drowned
but I have come to this shore for the hard wind

that flings waves high, smashes them against
the red lighthouse. I clutch my coat at the throat,
bend as the wind tears at my hair.

        Once, in the Amazon, far up the Napo River,
my spirit was cleansed by a Kichwa shaman.

I sat, eyes closed, hands in my lap, as he blew
smoke from a fat twist of tobacco held tight in his teeth
and swirled it around my body with a bundle of leaves.

The leaves grazed my hair, my face as he spun
whatever darkness was within me up into the bundle,
like winding silk from the comb-footed spiders.

Then, he padded to his doorway and shook the leaves
out into the jungle like a feather duster. After returning

he patted the air back around my shape and whistled
two notes over and over.

        Here, at the lake, warning flags snap, fly rigid.
My eyes water. The wind scours me. Empty swings clang.

Brontide

Greek for a low sound like distant thunder
but caused by faint earth tremors

The pond is alive in chirrs and creaks, deep-throated
twangs as frogs send their longings into the night.

From our porch I lean out to peer above the black
tree line as light rockets up, bursts into shimmery globes

then shatters like dandelion seed heads. Muffled booms
boom in the next county, setting off a surge of insect grinds

and ratchetings in the dark. We've lived in this house
only a week, having moved from forty years in another state.

Another life. Stacks of flattened cardboard, piles of boxes
still sealed in every room. Bone weary, dizzy-sick. Lost.

We know none of the neighbors. My husband calls me
to the bathroom window where the holiday blooms

above another town we can't name. His hand steadies
my shoulder while we stare off imagining folks way out there

on their distant blankets, children covering their ears;
every faraway unfamiliar face aglow beneath showers of light.

Gluggaveður

Icelandic for "window weather," meaning
a pleasant-looking but bitterly cold day

Sharp blue sky and snow sequined in sunlight. It's window
weather but it isn't cold that keeps me cocooned at my window.

In Madrid, confined in their apartments, people play Bingo.
A shout: *trenta y tres!* The game resumes through windows.

Virtual school each day at the kitchen table, computer
screens frame each student in a Zoom window.

Sticky fingers splay on a pane of glass where Nana's
hand presses against the care home window.

Graduates cruise through town in a parade, honking,
waving. Happiness balloons from their car windows.

I think I'm becoming Edward Hopper's woman in
"Morning Sun" staring vacantly out her bedroom window.

Quarantined Italians sing each other out of loneliness,
arias float from balconies, opera booms from windows.

The sun drops lower, glints on the glass. A starling streaks
toward our house. Feathers remain, strewn on the window.

Sabsung

Thai word for the refreshment of
an exhausted mind and weary heart

The day moon floats in the high blue.
A paraglider circles, dips his bright wing.

Orange and yellow maple leaves drift,
spiral. Turkey buzzards skim bare branches

of the patchy woods and we begin
to end the year softly. See how the river stops

churning, opens here like welcoming hands.
For so long we've breathed little sips of air,

but in this moment of grace let us sigh
the paraglider into his wide turn,

watch him lower with the rose gold sun,
drop lightly to his feet, running on cool grass.

Psithurisma

*Greek for the continuous soft whisper
of pine trees in a breeze*

The hush-shush of pine needles is the sound
of trees gossiping and it's easy to believe

the pines know secrets, standing together for so long.
On the dappled forest floor a shrew pants

birthing four pups in a litter of decayed leaves,
and several horizons deeper, tree roots interlace

with hair-fine fungus. It's the gauzy network
hickory and beech trees use to care for their kin,

to deliver food to the young or sick. To the dying.
On the African savanna, clusters of acacia trees

pass warnings on the wind to others of their kind.
But these days, driving past a lone white oak in a field,

I wonder if it marks where the farmhouse stood,
where everyone gathered for lunch in its shade.

I think about the solitary ginkgo growing
by the sidewalk, fanning its leaves

because when you're rehearsing for the time
you'll live alone, what you see is all the empty sky.

Moksha

*Spiritual term in Hinduism for the soul's
liberation to a state of permanent bliss*

When everything starts over

there will be a blue sun
and you and I
will sway like the flowerings
on the floor of the sea.

There will be a new bird
and night will warm
our thoughts with twin
moons, will spread

and scent the ground. And you
and I will find mercy
painted on every stone. Rain
will sing its long song

and you and I. And you and I.

About the Author

Marion Starling Boyer's book, *Ice Hours*, was selected for the 2021 Wheelbarrow Books Poetry Prize, and was released in 2023 from Michigan State University Press, and mentioned in the February issue of *Poets & Writers* magazine as a "New and Noteworthy" book. Boyer is also the author of *The Sea Was Never Far* (Main Street Rag, 2019) and *The Clock of the Long Now* (Mayapple Press, 2009). She is a two-time winner of the Grayson Books Chapbook Contest; her collection *Composing the Rain* won and was published in 2014. Boyer is a Communication professor emerita from Kalamazoo Valley Community College and served on the board for Kalamazoo Poetry Fest. She now lives in Ohio and enjoys teaching writing workshops for Lit Cleveland and Lit Youngstown. Currently, Boyer is co-leading a series of reading workshops designed to encourage the reading of books by contemporary poets. For more, link to www.marionstarlingboyer.com.

Notes

Sources for *Cento for Mångata*:

Lee Young Lee, *Always A Rose*; Christina Beasley, *Rare Gifts*;
Elaine Seaman, *Falling Timbers*; Jack Ridl, *Keeping On, Raking
Leaves with the Gods in July*; James Scannell McCormick, *Three
Beaches*; Kathleen McGookey, *On a Scale of Zero to Ten*; Laura
Grace Weldon, *Call of the Void*; Jericho Brown, *Dear Whiteness*;
Brian Turner, *Alhazen of Basra, Cole's Guitar, Where Telemetries
End*; Christine Howey, *Destination Vacation, Meals*; Diane Seuss,
Rising, Viceroy; Tony Hoagland, *Beauty, Honda Pavarotti*;
William Stafford, *On Earth*; Patricia Smith, *A Colored Girl Will
Slice You If You Talk Wrong About Motown*; Bob Hickok,
Rothko's Last Meditation; Naomi Shahib Nye, *The Crossed-Out
Word*; Pattiann Rogers, *For the Wren Trapped in a Cathedral*.

Sources for *Cento for Yūgen*:

Astronomers: Galileo Galilei and Carl Sagan; Apollo Astronauts:
Neil Armstrong, Alan Bean, Roger B. Chaffee, Mike Collins,
James B. Irwin, Edgar Mitchell; Space Shuttle Astronauts:
Loren Acton, Willie McCool; Russian Cosmonaut Aleksei Leonov;
Astrophysicist Neil deGrasse Tyson, Poet Archibald MacLeish's
Voyage to the Moon, Epistle to be Left in the Earth.

Pronunciation Guide:

Adjal [ADD-jahl]
Boketto [bow-KET-oh]
Brontide [BRAWN-tide]
Buddhi [boo-DEE]
Culaccino [cool-ah-CHEE-no]
Forelsket [four- ELSE-ka]
Gluggaveður [GLOOG-ah-vether]
Iktsuarpok [eek-swaar-poke]
Komorebi [Ko-MORE-ab-bee]
L'Appel Du Vide [la pell due Veed]
Mångata [moon-GAT-ah]
Moksha [MOK-shah]
Nepakartojama [nay-KARTO-yama]
Nyepi [nn-YEH-pee]
Poronkusema [Pour-ron-KUTE-see-mah]
Psithurismsa [SITH-er-ISS-mah]
Sabsung [SOB-soog]
Saudade [so-DAH-day]
Tingo [TING-go]
Uitwaaien [out-VIE-ann]
Vedriti [Ven-DREE-tee]
Yoin [yoh-EEN]
Yr [Yrrr]
Yūgen [YOU-ghen]
Zwischenraum [ZVISH-ehn-houm]

Acknowledgments

It is with gratitude I wish to acknowledge and thank the editors of the following journals for publishing these poems, some in slightly different form.

Atlanta Review's 2021 International Poetry Contest finalist: "Nyepi."
Braided Way Magazine: "Yoin," "Buddhi."
Encore Magazine: "Brontide," "Moksha."
MacQueen's Quinterly: "Foresket."
Modern Haiku: "Vendriti."
Moth Orchid Press Haibun Anthology: "Iktsuarpok."
The Comstock Review: "Psithurisma."
The Orchards Poetry Journal: "Cento for Yūgen," "Cento for Mångata," "Gluggaveður."
Quartet: "Zwischenraum."
Sheila-Na-Gig: "L'Appel Du Vide," "Culaccino," "Komorebi," "Sabsung," "Uitwaaien."
Spoon River Poetry Journal: "Poronkusema."

Credit for the epigraph beginning the collection: Victoria Chang, excerpt from "Logic" from *Obit*. Copyright © 2020 Copper Canyon Press, coppercanyonepress.org.

I am deeply grateful to Joan Kwon Glass for selecting my chapbook as the winner of Grayson Books Chapbook Prize, for the untold hours and close attention she gave to making her decision and for her generous praise.

It is a privilege to work Ginny Connors who devotes herself to this outstanding press and to examining and polishing every fine detail of a manuscript to make it into a beautiful book. You have my admiration and my gratitude, Ginny.

Praise and appreciation for the cover photo provided by Barbara Sabol.

I lean on fellow poets to critique and help me craft my work. Heartfelt love and blessings on Ohio poet, Barbara Sabol, and Michigan poets, Kit Almy, Gail Griffin, Christine Horton, Gail Martin, Nancy Nott, and Susan Blackwell Ramsey for all their encouragement and wisdom.